ACHIEVING CLARITY AND FOCUS

STRATEGIES FOR LIVING MINDFULLY

DR. JAGADEESH PILLAI

Copyright © Dr. Jagadeesh Pillai
All Rights Reserved.

This book has been self-published with all reasonable efforts taken to make the material error-free by the author. No part of this book shall be used, reproduced in any manner whatsoever without written permission from the author, except in the case of brief quotations embodied in critical articles and reviews.

The Author of this book is solely responsible and liable for its content including but not limited to the views, representations, descriptions, statements, information, opinions and references ["Content"]. The Content of this book shall not constitute or be construed or deemed to reflect the opinion or expression of the Publisher or Editor. Neither the Publisher nor Editor endorse or approve the Content of this book or guarantee the reliability, accuracy or completeness of the Content published herein and do not make any representations or warranties of any kind, express or implied, including but not limited to the implied warranties of merchantability, fitness for a particular purpose. The Publisher and Editor shall not be liable whatsoever for any errors, omissions, whether such errors or omissions result from negligence, accident, or any other cause or claims for loss or damages of any kind, including without limitation, indirect or consequential loss or damage arising out of use, inability to use, or about the reliability, accuracy or sufficiency of the information contained in this book.

Made with ♥ on the Notion Press Platform
www.notionpress.com

|| Dedicated to all wisdom seekers around the World ||

৪৩

Contents

Prayer	*vii*
About The Author	*ix*
Preface	*xiii*
1. Introduction To Mindfulness	1
Part 1	
2. Exploring Mindfulness Practices	5
Part 2	
3. Developing A Mindful Lifestyle	11
Part 3	
4. Working Mindfully Through Difficult Situations	17
Part 4	
5. Mindfulness In Relationships	23
Part 5	
6. Mindful Parenting	29
Part 6	
7. Understanding Your Emotions With Mindfulness	35
Part 7	
8. The Benefits Of Being Mindful	41
Part 8	
9. Cultivating Gratitude In Mindfulness	47
Part 9	
10. Finding Balance Through Mindfulness	53
Part 10	
11. Enhancing Your Sleep With Mindfulness	59

Contents

Part 11

12. Practicing Mindfulness In Daily Life   65

Part 12

13. Mindful Eating   71

Part 13

14. Mindfulness For Stress Management   77

Part 14

15. Reaching Your Goals With Mindfulness   83

Part 15

Other Books Of The Author   89

Contact   97

PRAYER

Saraswati Namasthubhyam Varade Kamarupini

Vidyarambham Karishyami Siddhir Bavathume Sadha

Greetings to Devi Saraswati, the benevolent granter of blessings and fulfiller of desires. O Devi, as I embark on my studies, I humbly ask that you grant me the wisdom to comprehend correctly.

ॐ

ABOUT THE AUTHOR

Dr. Jagadeesh Pillai is a renowned Guinness World Record holder, writer, and researcher hailing from Varanasi, also known as the abode of Lord Shiva. With a Ph.D. in Vedic Science and a range of creative ideas and achievements, he is a true polymath. He is the author of more than 100 books including Research Publications. Although his roots can be traced back to Kerala, the people of Varanasi hold him in high regard and affectionately consider him one of their own.

In 1998, Dr. Pillai was offered a job at Banaras Hindu University, but he left the position after only two months to pursue greater goals in life. He believed that in order to study Indian scriptures and engage in other creative endeavours, he needed to retire from the daily grind of working solely for money at a young age.

He started an export business from scratch, using the knowledge he had gained from a previous job in the industry. His intelligence and unique approach to business led to great success in a short period of time, earning him more in just a decade and a half than he would have in a lifetime working in a government job. Upon the passing of Dr. APJ Abdul Kalam, Dr. Pillai decided to leave the business and dedicate himself to reading, studying, researching, and experimenting.

During his tenure in the export business, Dr. Pillai traveled to over 16 countries, gaining valuable insight and experiencing the world and life in detail.

ABOUT THE AUTHOR

Dr. Pillai has achieved four Guinness World Records in the following subjects:

"Script to Screen" - In this record, Dr. Pillai produced and directed an animation film within the shortest time possible, breaking the previous record set by Canadians. He has also received numerous national and international awards and recognitions for this achievement.

Longest Line of Postcards - For this record, Dr. Pillai created a line of 16,300 postcards on the occasion of the 163rd anniversary of Indian Postal Day. The event also included a questionnaire about the Indian flag.

Largest Poster Awareness Campaign - Dr. Pillai designed an awareness campaign on the subject of "Beti Bachao - Beti Padhao" (Save the Girl Child - Educate the Girl Child) to achieve this record.

Largest Envelope - In tribute to the Indian Prime Minister's "Make in India" initiative, Dr. Pillai created a 4000 square meter envelope using waste paper to achieve this record.

Attempted - **70000 Candles on a 210 kg Cake** - To celebrate the 70th Indian Independence Day, Dr. Pillai attempted to light 70,000 candles on a 210 kg cake, which was recorded in World Records India.

Attempted - **Documentary on Dhamek Stupa of Sarnath in 17 Languages** - Dr. Pillai attempted to create a documentary on the Dhamek Stupa of Sarnath, dubbing it in 17 different languages. The result of this attempt is currently awaiting

● x ●

ABOUT THE AUTHOR

confirmation from the Guinness World Records.

Dr. Pillai is skilled in teaching the Bhagavad Gita, a Hindu scripture, and is popular among young people. He has helped many young people improve their lives through his motivational teachings.

In addition to teaching, he has composed and sung numerous Sanskrit Bhajans and patriotic songs.

He has also written and directed several short films and documentaries for awareness campaigns, and has volunteered with the police in both UP and Kerala to spread awareness about various issues through videos and photography.

Incredibly, he has produced and directed over 100 documentaries about the city of Varanasi, all on his own.

He has also helped and guided more than 25 boys and girls to achieve world records through creative and innovative methods. He is a multifaceted person who uses his intellect and the blessings given to him by God to excel in various areas. He is both a teacher and a student, always learning and teaching, and is able to master any subject he comes across.

He is a selfless social activist and motivational speaker who has overcome struggles and failures to become a successful and enthusiastic individual with a rich life experience.

In addition to his work with the Bhagavad Gita, he is also an efficient Tarot card reader, Astro-Vastu consultant, and a talented singer and composer. He has sung the entire Ram Charita Manas and Bhagavad Gita in his own compositions, and has sung the phrase "Lokah Samastha Sukhino Bhavantu" in 50 different languages. He is currently working on a detailed and scientific study of Vedas, Upanishads, Puranas, and the Bhagavad Gita. He has also composed and sung the Hanuman Chalisa and Gayatri Mantra in 108 and 1008 different compositions, respectively.

Awards - Four Times Guinness World Records, Winner of Mahatma Gandhi Vishwa Shanti Puraskar, Mahatma Gandhi Global Peace Ambassador, Kashi Ratna Award, Dr. APJ Abdul Kalam Motivational Person of the Year 2017, Mother Teresa Award, Indira Gandhi Priyadarshini Award, Bharat Vikas Ratna Award, Udyog Ratna Award, Vigyan Prasar Award, Poorvanchal Ratn Samman.

Preface

In today's world, it can be difficult to stay focused and maintain clarity amidst the hustle and bustle of everyday life. Achieving Clarity and Focus: Strategies for Living Mindfully is a book that provides readers with the tools and strategies they need to live a mindful life. Through this book, readers will learn how to cultivate clarity and focus in their lives, allowing them to live with intention and purpose.

This book is designed to help readers gain a better understanding of the power of mindfulness and how it can be used to create a more meaningful life. It provides readers with practical strategies and techniques to help them stay focused and clear-minded in the midst of life's distractions. Readers will learn how to cultivate a mindful attitude, how to practice mindfulness in their daily lives, and how to use mindfulness to create a more meaningful life.

Achieving Clarity and Focus: Strategies for Living Mindfully is an invaluable resource for anyone looking to live a more mindful life. It is written in an accessible and engaging style, making it easy to understand and apply the strategies and techniques presented. This book is a must-read for anyone looking to gain clarity and focus in their lives and to live with intention and purpose.

I

Introduction to Mindfulness

Mindfulness is a practice of being aware of the present moment and accepting it without judgment. It is a way of living that encourages us to be aware of our thoughts, feelings, and physical sensations in order to gain insight into our lives. Mindfulness can help us to become more aware of our thoughts and feelings, and to be more present in our lives.

The first step in introducing mindfulness is to understand the concept. Mindfulness is not about trying to control or change our thoughts and feelings, but rather to observe them without judgment. It is important to recognize that our thoughts and feelings are not necessarily true or accurate, and that we can choose to respond to them in a mindful way.

The next step is to practice mindfulness. This can be done

through meditation, yoga, or other activities that help us to be present in the moment. It is important to remember that mindfulness is not about trying to control our thoughts and feelings, but rather to observe them without judgment.

Finally, it is important to recognize that mindfulness is a practice that takes time and effort. It is not something that can be achieved overnight, but rather something that requires dedication and commitment. With practice, we can learn to be more mindful and to live more fully in the present moment.

By introducing mindfulness in this chapter, readers will gain a better understanding of the concept and how to practice it. They will also learn how to be more present in their lives and to gain insight into their thoughts and feelings. With this knowledge, readers will be able to live more mindfully and to achieve clarity and focus in their lives.

"The key to living mindfully is to focus on the present moment and be aware of your thoughts and feelings."

৪৩

II

Exploring Mindfulness Practices

Mindfulness is a concept that has been around for centuries, but has only recently gained widespread popularity in Western cultures. The reason for this is simple – mindfulness is a powerful tool for helping people achieve greater clarity and focus in their lives. However, mindfulness is not just a single practice or technique, but rather an umbrella term that encompasses many different methods and techniques for achieving greater awareness and presence. In this chapter, we will explore some of the most popular mindfulness practices, so that you can choose the ones that work best for you.

Mindful Breathing

One of the most fundamental mindfulness practices is

mindful breathing. This simple exercise involves focusing on your breath as you inhale and exhale, allowing your mind to become calm and focused. To practice mindful breathing, simply find a quiet place to sit, close your eyes, and focus your attention on your breath. As you inhale, try to feel the air entering your nose and filling your lungs. As you exhale, try to feel the air leaving your body. This simple exercise is an excellent way to start your mindfulness practice, and can be done anywhere, at any time.

Mindful Meditation

Mindful meditation is another popular mindfulness practice that involves sitting in a quiet place and focusing on your breath. However, in this practice, you take it one step further by focusing on your thoughts as well. As you inhale and exhale, try to observe your thoughts without judgment. If your mind starts to wander, simply bring your attention back to your breath. This practice is designed to help you become more aware of your thoughts and feelings, and to cultivate greater peace and calm in your mind.

Body Scan Meditation

The body scan meditation is another popular mindfulness practice that involves becoming more aware of your body. This practice is usually done lying down, but can also be done sitting or standing. To practice the body scan, start at the top of your head and slowly scan down your body, noticing any sensations or feelings in each part of your body. As you scan down your body, try to release any tension or discomfort that you may be feeling. This practice is a great way to reduce stress and increase relaxation.

Walking Meditation

Walking meditation is a mindfulness practice that involves walking in a slow, deliberate manner, focusing on each step as you take it. To practice walking meditation, simply find a quiet place to walk, and start walking slowly, focusing on the sensation of each step as you take it. You can also focus on your breath or on your surroundings, taking in the sights and sounds around you. Walking meditation is a great way to practice mindfulness in motion, and can be done anywhere, at any time.

Yoga

Yoga is another mindfulness practice that has become very popular in recent years. Yoga is a physical practice that involves moving your body through a series of poses, while also focusing on your breath. By doing so, you cultivate greater awareness and presence, both in your body and in your mind. There are many different styles of yoga, so you can choose the one that works best for you. Whether you prefer a slow and gentle style, or a more energetic and challenging style, yoga is an excellent way to practice mindfulness and increase your focus and clarity.

In this chapter, we have explored some of the most popular mindfulness practices, including mindful breathing, mindful meditation, body scan meditation, walking meditation, and yoga. By incorporating these practices into your daily routine, you can cultivate greater clarity and focus in your life, and experience greater peace and calm. Whether you are a beginner or an experienced practitioner, these mindfulness practices can help you achieve your goals and live a more fulfilling life.

"Clarity of thought comes from taking the time to reflect and be mindful of your actions."

&

III

Developing a Mindful Lifestyle

Now that you have a better understanding of mindfulness practices, it's time to explore how you can integrate these practices into your daily life to achieve a more mindful lifestyle. A mindful lifestyle is characterized by greater awareness, presence, and focus in all aspects of your life, from your work and relationships to your health and well-being. In this chapter, we will explore some key strategies for developing a mindful lifestyle.

Making Mindfulness a Priority

The first step in developing a mindful lifestyle is to make mindfulness a priority in your life. This means setting aside time each day to practice mindfulness and incorporating mindfulness into your daily activities. You can start by setting aside just a few minutes each day to practice mindfulness, and gradually increasing this amount of time as you become more comfortable with the practice. You can also try incorporating mindfulness into your daily activities, such as paying attention to your breath while you drive or focusing on your thoughts and feelings while you eat.

Finding Balance

Another key aspect of developing a mindful lifestyle is finding balance. This means balancing your physical, emotional, mental, and spiritual needs in a way that supports your overall well-being. To find balance, it's important to prioritize self-care and make time for activities that bring you joy and fulfillment. This may include exercise, spending time with friends and family, and engaging in hobbies and interests. By finding balance in your life, you can reduce stress and cultivate greater peace and happiness.

Managing Stress

Stress is a natural part of life, but it can have a negative impact on your well-being if it is not managed effectively. To manage stress, it's important to identify the sources of stress in your life and develop strategies for reducing or eliminating these stressors. Mindfulness practices, such as mindful breathing and meditation, can help you manage stress and reduce its negative impact on your life. Additionally, it's important to take breaks and engage in self-care, such as exercise and relaxation, to reduce stress and improve your overall well-being.

Living in the Moment

Living in the moment is another key aspect of developing a mindful lifestyle. This means focusing on the present moment, rather than dwelling on the past or worrying about the future. To live in the moment, it's important to cultivate awareness of your thoughts, feelings, and sensations, and to observe them without judgment. Mindfulness practices, such as mindful breathing and meditation, can help you cultivate greater awareness and presence in the moment. Additionally, it's important to be intentional about your actions and to focus on the task at hand, rather than letting your mind wander.

Embracing a Growth Mindset

Finally, it's important to embrace a growth mindset when developing a mindful lifestyle. A growth mindset means being open to learning and growing, and embracing challenges as opportunities for growth. By embracing a growth mindset, you can cultivate greater resilience, optimism, and well-being, and achieve greater clarity and focus in your life.

In this chapter, we have explored some key strategies for developing a mindful lifestyle, including making mindfulness a priority, finding balance, managing stress, living in the moment, and embracing a growth mindset. By incorporating these strategies into your daily life, you can cultivate greater awareness, presence, and focus, and experience greater peace and happiness. Whether you are just starting your mindfulness journey, or are an experienced practitioner, these strategies will help you achieve your goals and live a more fulfilling life.

"Focus on the present and be mindful of your goals to achieve clarity and purpose."

IV

Working Mindfully Through Difficult Situations

Difficult situations are an inevitable part of life, and they can challenge our well-being and disrupt our sense of peace and happiness. However, by developing a mindful approach to these challenges, we can work through them with greater clarity and focus, and emerge stronger and more resilient. In this chapter, we will explore some key strategies for working mindfully through difficult situations.

Recognizing Your Emotions

The first step in working mindfully through difficult situations is to recognize your emotions. This means becoming aware of the thoughts and feelings that arise in response to challenging situations, and observing them without judgment. By recognizing your emotions, you can gain a better understanding of how you are responding to challenges, and take steps to manage your emotions in a healthy way.

Practicing Self-Compassion

Self-compassion is an important aspect of working mindfully through difficult situations. This means treating yourself with kindness and understanding, even when you are struggling or feeling overwhelmed. To practice self-compassion, it's important to be gentle with yourself, and to avoid self-criticism or judgment. Additionally, it's important to take care of yourself and engage in self-care activities, such as exercise, relaxation, and spending time with loved ones.

Mindful Breathing

Mindful breathing is another key strategy for working mindfully through difficult situations. By focusing on your breath and cultivating awareness of your thoughts and feelings, you can reduce stress and anxiety, and cultivate a sense of calm and peace. Mindful breathing can be practiced in any situation, and can help you remain calm and focused, even in the midst of challenging circumstances.

Mindful Thinking

Mindful thinking is another key strategy for working mindfully through difficult situations. This means being intentional about your thoughts, and focusing on the present moment, rather than dwelling on the past or worrying about the future. To practice mindful thinking, it's important to observe your thoughts without judgment, and to redirect your attention to the present moment when your mind begins to wander. Additionally, it's important to engage in positive self-talk, and to focus on thoughts and feelings that promote well-being and resilience.

Seeking Support

Finally, it's important to seek support when working through difficult situations. This means reaching out to loved ones, friends, or a mental health professional for help and guidance. By seeking support, you can gain a different perspective on your challenges, and receive the encouragement and support you need to work through them in a healthy and positive way.

In this chapter, we have explored some key strategies for working mindfully through difficult situations, including recognizing your emotions, practicing self-compassion, mindful breathing, mindful thinking, and seeking support. By incorporating these strategies into your life, you can cultivate a more mindful and resilient approach to challenges, and achieve greater clarity and focus, even in the midst of difficult circumstances. Whether you are facing a minor setback or a major life challenge, these strategies will help you work through difficult situations with greater awareness and presence, and emerge stronger and more resilient.

"Living mindfully is about being aware of your thoughts and feelings and taking action to reach your goals."

೮೦

V

Mindfulness in Relationships

Relationships play a significant role in our lives, providing us with emotional support, love, and connection. However, relationships can also be a source of stress, conflict, and frustration. By incorporating mindfulness into our relationships, we can cultivate greater clarity, focus, and empathy, and work through challenges with greater ease and grace. In this chapter, we will explore the benefits of mindfulness in relationships, and provide strategies for cultivating mindful relationships.

The Benefits of Mindfulness in Relationships

There are numerous benefits to incorporating mindfulness into our relationships, including improved communication, reduced stress and conflict, and increased empathy and understanding. When we are mindful in our relationships, we are more present and attentive to our partner's needs and feelings, which can help to strengthen the bond between us. Additionally, mindfulness can help us to manage our emotions and reactions in challenging situations, which can reduce stress and conflict, and promote a more harmonious and fulfilling relationship.

Cultivating Mindful Communication

Mindful communication is a key component of mindful relationships. This means being present and attentive when communicating with your partner, and actively listening to their thoughts and feelings. To cultivate mindful communication, it's important to avoid distractions and engage in active listening, which involves paying attention to what your partner is saying, and responding in a supportive and understanding manner. Additionally, it's important to communicate openly and honestly, and to express your thoughts and feelings in a clear and non-judgmental way.

Practicing Empathy

Empathy is another important aspect of mindfulness in relationships. This means putting yourself in your partner's shoes, and imagining how they might be feeling. By practicing empathy, you can develop a deeper understanding of your partner's perspective, and respond to their needs and feelings in a supportive and compassionate way. Additionally, empathy can help to reduce stress and conflict, and promote a greater sense of connection and intimacy in your relationship.

Managing Conflict

Conflict is an inevitable part of relationships, and it can be challenging to manage in the heat of the moment. However, by incorporating mindfulness into your approach to conflict, you can work through challenges with greater ease and clarity. To manage conflict mindfully, it's important to take a step back, breathe, and become aware of your thoughts and feelings. Additionally, it's important to communicate openly and honestly, and to listen to your partner's perspective with an open mind. By managing conflict mindfully, you can reduce stress and promote a more harmonious relationship.

Celebrating Differences

In any relationship, it's important to celebrate differences, rather than trying to change your partner. By embracing your partner's unique perspectives, experiences, and values, you can promote greater understanding and connection, and reduce stress and conflict. Additionally, by celebrating your partner's differences, you can promote a greater sense of individuality and autonomy, which is essential for a healthy and fulfilling relationship.

In this chapter, we have explored the benefits of mindfulness in relationships, and provided strategies for cultivating mindful relationships, including mindful communication, practicing empathy, managing conflict, and celebrating differences. By incorporating these strategies into your relationships, you can cultivate greater clarity, focus, and empathy, and work through challenges with greater ease and grace. Whether you are in a romantic relationship, a friendship, or a familial relationship, mindfulness can help you to strengthen your connections and promote a more fulfilling and harmonious life.

"Achieving clarity and focus requires dedication and commitment to living in the present moment."

VI

Mindful Parenting

Parenting is one of the most rewarding and challenging experiences in life. It requires a great deal of patience, empathy, and emotional intelligence. Mindful parenting is a way of approaching the role of a parent with awareness, compassion, and non-judgment. By incorporating mindfulness into your parenting style, you can enhance your relationship with your children, foster their emotional well-being, and help them develop important life skills.

What is Mindful Parenting?

Mindful parenting is a practice that involves bringing awareness to the present moment in your interactions with your children. It is about becoming aware of your thoughts, feelings, and behaviors, and how they impact your child. Mindful parenting also involves being non-judgmental, compassionate, and empathetic towards your child and yourself.

Benefits of Mindful Parenting

Improved Emotional Intelligence: By practicing mindfulness, you can become more self-aware, which can help you better understand and manage your emotions. This can improve your emotional intelligence, and make you better equipped to handle challenging situations.

Stronger Parent-Child Bond: Mindful parenting can help you develop a stronger, more authentic relationship with your child. By being fully present in your interactions, you can create a deeper emotional connection with your child and better understand their needs.

Increased Empathy: By practicing mindfulness, you can become more empathetic and compassionate towards your child. This can help you to better understand their feelings and perspectives, and respond in a way that is supportive and nurturing.

Improved Communication:

Mindful parenting can help you to communicate more effectively with your child. By being fully present and non-judgmental in your conversations, you can create a safe and supportive environment that encourages open and honest communication.

Reduced Stress and Anxiety:

Mindful parenting can help to reduce stress and anxiety, as it allows you to focus on the present moment and prioritize self-care. This can also help you to respond to challenging situations in a more calm and centered way.

How to Practice Mindful Parenting

Be present: Make an effort to be fully present in your interactions with your children. Put aside distractions and focus on the moment at hand.

Practice non-judgment: Try to approach your child and their behavior with non-judgment. Instead of being critical, offer them empathy and understanding.

Pay attention to your breathing: Take a few deep breaths before responding to your child. This can help you to calm your mind and respond in a more centered way.

Engage in mindfulness activities: Encourage your child to practice mindfulness activities with you, such as meditation, yoga, or deep breathing exercises.

Take care of yourself: Prioritize self-care and make time for activities that help you feel refreshed and recharged.

In conclusion, mindful parenting is a powerful tool for enhancing the parent-child relationship and fostering the emotional well-being of your child. By incorporating mindfulness into your parenting style, you can create a supportive, understanding, and loving environment that can help your child to flourish and grow.

"Living mindfully is about being aware of your thoughts and feelings and taking action to reach your goals."

∞

VII

Understanding Your Emotions with Mindfulness

Mindfulness is a powerful tool that can help individuals develop a greater understanding and awareness of their emotions. When we engage in mindfulness practices, we learn to observe our thoughts and feelings without judgment, and to respond to them in a healthy and productive manner. This can have a significant impact on our mental and emotional well-being, and can help us navigate the ups and downs of life with greater ease.

One of the key benefits of mindfulness is that it can help us develop greater self-awareness. When we are mindful, we pay attention to our emotions and thoughts as they arise, without getting caught up in them. This allows us to gain a better understanding of what drives our reactions and behaviors, and to identify patterns that may be hindering our ability to live life to the fullest.

For example, if you find yourself feeling overwhelmed or stressed, mindfulness can help you identify the root cause of these feelings. You may find that you are taking on too much at once, or that you have unrealistic expectations of yourself. Once you understand what is driving these feelings, you can then take steps to address the root cause and find a more sustainable way of living.

Another benefit of mindfulness is that it can help you develop a greater sense of emotional regulation. When you are mindful, you become more aware of your emotions as they arise, and you learn to respond to them in a calm and centered manner. This can help you reduce stress and anxiety, and increase feelings of joy and peace.

For example, if you find yourself feeling angry or frustrated, mindfulness can help you identify the triggers for these emotions and provide you with tools to manage them. This might involve taking a few deep breaths, practicing mindful breathing exercises, or using visualization techniques to calm your mind and body.

Mindfulness can also help you develop better relationships with others. By being more aware of your own emotions and thoughts, you become better equipped to understand the perspectives of others and to communicate more effectively. This can help you to resolve conflicts, build stronger relationships, and create a more harmonious environment for yourself and those around you.

For example, if you find yourself struggling in a particular relationship, mindfulness can help you identify the triggers for conflict and help you to communicate more effectively with the other person. This might involve focusing on active listening, expressing your feelings in a non-judgmental manner, and working to find common ground.

Finally, mindfulness can help you to cultivate greater resilience in the face of life's challenges. By becoming more aware of your emotions and thoughts, and learning to respond to them in a healthy and productive manner, you develop greater emotional intelligence and emotional stability. This can help you to cope with difficult situations, such as illness, loss, or financial stress, in a more effective and positive way.

In conclusion, mindfulness is a powerful tool for understanding and managing your emotions. By incorporating mindfulness practices into your daily life, you can develop greater self-awareness, emotional regulation, and resilience, and build stronger relationships with others. Whether you are dealing with stress, anxiety, or difficult life situations, mindfulness can provide you with the tools you need to achieve clarity and focus, and to live life to the fullest.

"Focus on the present and be mindful of your intentions to achieve clarity and purpose."

VIII

The Benefits of Being Mindful

In today's fast-paced world, it's easy to get caught up in the constant rush of responsibilities and distractions. This can lead to feelings of stress, anxiety, and a lack of fulfillment in life. Fortunately, mindfulness offers a solution to this problem by helping individuals develop a clearer and more focused mind.

The practice of mindfulness involves paying attention to the present moment and being aware of your thoughts, feelings, and sensations without judgment. By doing this, individuals are able to gain a better understanding of themselves and their emotions, and develop a greater sense of clarity and focus in their daily lives.

In this chapter, we will explore the many benefits of being mindful and how incorporating mindfulness practices into your daily routine can improve your overall well-being.

Reduced Stress and Anxiety

One of the most notable benefits of mindfulness is its ability to reduce stress and anxiety. By focusing on the present moment, individuals are able to let go of worries and fears about the future, and instead live in the here and now. This shift in perspective can help to ease feelings of stress and anxiety, leading to a more peaceful and fulfilling life.

Improved Emotional Regulation

Another benefit of mindfulness is that it can help individuals regulate their emotions. By paying attention to their thoughts and feelings, individuals are able to identify patterns of negative thoughts and emotions, and develop new, more positive patterns of thinking. This can lead to a greater sense of emotional balance and stability, and a reduction in feelings of anger, sadness, and frustration.

Increased Mental Clarity

Mindfulness practices can also help individuals to increase their mental clarity. By focusing on the present moment, individuals are able to free their minds from distractions, and allow their thoughts to become clearer and more focused. This can lead to improved decision-making, increased productivity, and a greater sense of purpose and direction in life.

Better Physical Health

In addition to its mental health benefits, mindfulness has also been shown to improve physical health. Research has found that mindfulness practices can help to reduce chronic pain, lower blood pressure, and improve sleep quality. By taking care of their physical health, individuals can improve their overall sense of well-being, and feel more energized and capable of tackling the challenges of daily life.

Stronger Relationships

Finally, mindfulness can also help individuals to strengthen their relationships. By being more present and aware in their interactions with others, individuals are able to develop deeper, more meaningful connections with those around them. This can lead to greater empathy and understanding, and a reduction in conflict and misunderstandings.

In conclusion, the benefits of being mindful are numerous and far-reaching. By incorporating mindfulness practices into your daily routine, you can improve your mental and physical health, develop stronger relationships, and achieve greater clarity and focus in your life. With its many benefits, mindfulness is truly a tool for creating a happier, more fulfilling life.

"Living mindfully is about being aware of your thoughts and feelings and taking action to reach your goals."

౮

IX

Cultivating Gratitude in Mindfulness

Gratitude is a powerful tool for cultivating mindfulness and a positive outlook on life. When we focus on what we are thankful for, we can shift our perspective away from negative thoughts and emotions, and towards a more optimistic and peaceful state of mind. In this chapter, we will explore how incorporating gratitude into our mindfulness practice can lead to greater clarity, focus, and overall well-being.

What is Gratitude?

Gratitude is the practice of acknowledging and appreciating the good things in our lives. It involves recognizing the positive aspects of our experiences and taking the time to acknowledge and express gratitude for them. This can range from the simple things in life, such as a warm bed to sleep in or a delicious meal, to more significant aspects, such as supportive friends and family, good health, and meaningful work.

How Gratitude Enhances Mindfulness

Mindfulness is about being present in the moment and paying attention to our thoughts, feelings, and surroundings. When we practice gratitude, we focus our attention on what is good in our lives, which helps us to remain in the present moment and be mindful of our experiences. This shift in focus can lead to an increased sense of calm and well-being, as well as reducing the negative impact of stress and anxiety.

Gratitude also helps us to cultivate a positive outlook on life, which can impact our overall sense of happiness and fulfillment. By focusing on the good things in our lives, we are less likely to become caught up in negative thoughts and emotions, and instead develop a more resilient and optimistic mindset.

Ways to Incorporate Gratitude into Your Mindfulness Practice

There are many ways to incorporate gratitude into your mindfulness practice, and the key is to find what works best for you. Here are some tips to get started:

Keep a Gratitude Journal: Write down a few things that you are thankful for each day. This can be as simple as listing a few items, or you can write more detailed reflections on what you are grateful for and why.

Take a Gratitude Walk: Take a walk and focus on the things you are thankful for in your environment. This can be the beauty of nature, a kind gesture from a stranger, or simply the opportunity to get some exercise.

Practice Gratitude Meditation: Sit quietly and focus on your breath. Then, bring to mind things that you are thankful for and allow yourself to feel a sense of gratitude for each one.

Share Your Gratitude: Share your gratitude with others, either in person or through social media. This can help to spread positivity and bring a sense of community to your gratitude practice.

Incorporating gratitude into your mindfulness practice is an excellent way to cultivate a more positive outlook on life and reduce stress and anxiety. It is a simple, yet powerful tool that can lead to greater happiness, fulfillment, and overall well-being.

In conclusion, gratitude is an essential aspect of mindfulness that can enhance your practice and lead to greater clarity and focus. By taking the time to acknowledge and appreciate the good things in our lives, we can cultivate a more positive and resilient mindset, and improve our overall well-being.

"Living mindfully is about being aware of your thoughts and feelings and taking action to reach your goals."

৪০

X

Finding Balance Through Mindfulness

In our fast-paced and ever-changing world, it can be easy to feel overwhelmed and unbalanced. Stress, anxiety, and burnout are common experiences for many people, and it can be challenging to find a sense of peace and calm amidst the chaos. This is where mindfulness can be a valuable tool for finding balance in our lives. In this chapter, we will explore how mindfulness can help us to find balance and live more mindfully.

What is Mindful Balance?

Mindful balance refers to the state of being present and fully engaged in each moment, without being overly attached to our thoughts and emotions. It involves a harmonious integration of body, mind, and spirit, allowing us to approach life with a sense of calm and equanimity. Mindful balance means being fully aware of our experiences and being able to respond to them in a healthy and effective way, rather than being ruled by them.

How Mindfulness Supports Balance

Mindfulness supports balance by helping us to cultivate a more present and non-reactive state of mind. When we are mindful, we are able to become more aware of our thoughts, feelings, and experiences, allowing us to respond to them in a more balanced and effective way. This increased self-awareness can help us to identify unhelpful patterns of thought and behavior, and to make more intentional choices in our lives.

Mindfulness also helps us to develop a more resilient mindset, which is essential for finding balance in our lives. When we are mindful, we are less likely to be swayed by our emotions and thoughts, and instead develop a more grounded and centered approach to life. This can lead to a greater sense of well-being and a reduction in stress and anxiety.

Ways to Cultivate Mindful Balance

There are many ways to cultivate mindful balance in our lives, and the key is to find what works best for you. Here are some tips to get started:

Mindful Breathing: Take a few minutes each day to focus on your breath and bring your mind back to the present moment. This can help to calm your mind and reduce stress and anxiety.

Mindful Movement: Incorporate mindful movement into your daily routine, such as yoga, tai chi, or a simple walk in nature. This can help to improve your physical and mental balance.

Mindful Meditation: Practice mindfulness meditation regularly, such as sitting meditation or a guided body scan. This can help to develop a more present and non-reactive state of mind.

Mindful Self-Care: Take care of your physical, emotional, and mental health through activities such as exercise, healthy eating, and adequate sleep. This can help to improve your overall sense of well-being and balance.

Incorporating mindfulness into your daily life can be an effective way to cultivate balance and well-being. By taking the time to cultivate a more present and grounded state of mind, we can approach life with a greater sense of equanimity and resilience, and find a sense of peace amidst the chaos.

In conclusion, finding balance through mindfulness is a valuable tool for living mindfully and improving our overall well-being. By taking the time to cultivate a more present and non-reactive state of mind, we can approach life with greater balance, resilience, and peace, and find a sense of calm amidst the chaos.

"Focus on the present and be mindful of your intentions to achieve clarity and purpose in life."

XI

Enhancing Your Sleep with Mindfulness

Getting enough sleep is essential for our overall health and well-being, but for many people, it can be a challenge. Stress, anxiety, and other factors can interfere with our sleep patterns, leading to poor sleep quality and increased fatigue. In this chapter, we will explore how mindfulness can help to enhance our sleep and improve our overall health and well-being.

Why is Sleep Important?

Sleep is crucial for our physical and mental health. During sleep, our bodies have an opportunity to rest and rejuvenate, and our minds have a chance to process information and consolidate memories. Adequate sleep is essential for maintaining a healthy immune system, regulating our mood, and reducing stress and anxiety.

What is Mindful Sleep?

Mindful sleep is the practice of being aware and present during the sleep process. It involves paying attention to our thoughts, feelings, and physical sensations, and approaching them with compassion and non-judgment. The goal of mindful sleep is to improve sleep quality, reduce stress and anxiety, and enhance our overall well-being.

How to Practice Mindful Sleep

Here are some tips for practicing mindful sleep:

Establish a consistent sleep schedule: Try to go to bed and wake up at the same time every day, even on weekends. This helps to regulate our circadian rhythm and improve sleep quality.

Create a relaxing sleep environment: Make sure your bedroom is cool, quiet, and dark, and invest in a comfortable mattress and pillows.

Practice mindfulness during the day: Engage in daily mindfulness practices, such as meditation or yoga, to help reduce stress and improve sleep quality.

Reduce stimulants before bed: Avoid caffeine, alcohol, and nicotine in the hours leading up to bedtime, as these can interfere with sleep.

Wind down before bed: Engage in relaxing activities, such as reading or taking a bath, to help you relax and prepare for sleep.

Focus on the present moment: Pay attention to your thoughts, feelings, and physical sensations as you drift off to sleep. If your mind begins to race, take a deep breath and return your focus to the present moment.

Practice self-compassion: Treat yourself with kindness and understanding, and avoid negative self-talk if you have trouble sleeping.

In conclusion, enhancing your sleep with mindfulness can help to improve sleep quality and reduce stress and anxiety. By focusing on the present moment and paying attention to our thoughts, feelings, and physical sensations during the sleep process, we can develop a deeper understanding of ourselves and achieve greater well-being. With regular practice, mindful sleep can become a habit, helping us to live more mindfully and achieve greater health and happiness.

"Living mindfully is about being aware of your thoughts and feelings and taking action to reach your goals and aspirations."

XII

Practicing Mindfulness in Daily Life

Mindfulness is a powerful tool for cultivating clarity and focus in our lives, but it can be challenging to make it a part of our daily routine. The key to making mindfulness a part of our daily life is to start small and be consistent. In this chapter, we will explore practical ways to incorporate mindfulness into your daily routine and make it a habit.

What is Mindfulness?

Mindfulness is the practice of being fully present and engaged in each moment, without judgment. It involves paying attention to our thoughts, feelings, and experiences in a non-reactive way, allowing us to approach life with a sense of calm and equanimity. Mindfulness is not just a state of mind, but a way of being, and it can be cultivated through regular practice.

Why Practice Mindfulness in Daily Life?

There are many benefits to practicing mindfulness in daily life, including:

Improved mental health: Mindfulness has been shown to reduce stress and anxiety, and to improve mood and overall mental health.

Increased focus and productivity: By being more present and engaged in each moment, we can improve our focus and productivity in all areas of our lives.

Better relationships: Mindfulness can help us to improve our communication skills and build stronger, more meaningful relationships.

Greater self-awareness: Through mindfulness, we can become more aware of our thoughts, feelings, and experiences, allowing us to respond to them in a healthier and more effective way.

Improved physical health: Mindfulness has been shown to have a positive impact on physical health, including reducing symptoms of chronic pain and improving sleep quality.

How to Incorporate Mindfulness into Daily Life

Here are some practical tips for incorporating mindfulness into your daily routine:

Start small: Begin by practicing mindfulness for just a few minutes each day, and gradually increase the amount of time you spend practicing.

Make it a habit: Make mindfulness a part of your daily routine, such as practicing mindfulness breathing or meditation in the morning or before bed.

Bring mindfulness into your daily activities: Incorporate mindfulness into your daily activities, such as mindful eating, walking, or showering.

Use reminders: Set reminders throughout the day to practice mindfulness, such as a note on your phone or a reminder on your computer.

Find a mindfulness community: Join a local mindfulness group or participate in online mindfulness communities to stay motivated and connected to others who are also practicing mindfulness.

Incorporating mindfulness into your daily life is a gradual process, but with time and consistency, it can become a habit and a valuable tool for cultivating clarity and focus.

In conclusion, practicing mindfulness in daily life is an effective way to cultivate clarity, focus, and well-being. By taking the time to be fully present and engaged in each moment, we can approach life with a sense of calm and equanimity, and find peace amidst the chaos. With consistent practice, mindfulness can become a habit, allowing us to live more mindfully and improve all areas of our lives.

ა

"Achieving clarity and focus requires a conscious effort to stay in the present moment and be mindful of your actions."

૪૭

XIII
Mindful Eating

Eating is an essential aspect of our daily lives, but it can also be a source of stress, anxiety, and mindless behavior. In this chapter, we will explore the concept of mindful eating and how it can help us achieve clarity and focus in our lives.

What is Mindful Eating?

Mindful eating is the practice of being fully present and engaged while eating, paying attention to our thoughts, feelings, and physical sensations. It involves being mindful of our food choices, how we eat, and why we eat. The goal of mindful eating is to develop a deeper understanding of our relationship with food, and to cultivate a sense of peace and well-being while eating.

Why Practice Mindful Eating?

There are many benefits to practicing mindful eating, including:

Improved health: Mindful eating can help us make healthier food choices, and can improve our overall physical health.

Reduced stress and anxiety: Mindful eating can reduce stress and anxiety by helping us to slow down and be present in the moment.

Improved digestion: By being mindful while eating, we can improve our digestion and reduce symptoms of indigestion and bloating.

Better relationships with food: Mindful eating can help us to develop a healthier relationship with food, reducing the negative impact of emotional eating and binge eating.

Increased enjoyment of food: By being mindful while eating, we can appreciate the flavors, textures, and aromas of our food, increasing our enjoyment and satisfaction with eating.

How to Practice Mindful Eating

Here are some tips for practicing mindful eating:

Start by setting aside distractions: Turn off your phone and other electronic devices, and create a peaceful and distraction-free environment while eating.

Pay attention to your food: Take time to appreciate the look, smell, and taste of your food, and savor each bite.

Eat slowly: Chew your food thoroughly, and take breaks

between bites to notice your fullness.

Be aware of your thoughts and feelings: Notice any negative thoughts or emotions that may arise while eating, and approach them with kindness and compassion.

Practice gratitude: Before eating, take a moment to reflect on the food you have and the effort that went into producing it.

Use your senses: Engage all of your senses while eating, noticing the colors, textures, and flavors of your food.

Mindful eating is a powerful tool for cultivating clarity and focus in our lives, and it can be practiced in any setting, from formal meals to snacking on the go. With practice, mindful eating can become a habit, allowing us to approach food and eating with a sense of peace and well-being.

In conclusion, mindful eating is a valuable tool for improving our relationship with food and cultivating clarity and focus in our lives. By taking the time to be fully present and engaged while eating, we can reduce stress and anxiety, improve our physical health, and find joy and peace in our relationship with food. With regular practice, mindful eating can become a habit, helping us to live more mindfully and achieve greater well-being.

"Living mindfully is about being aware of your thoughts and feelings and taking action to reach your goals and dreams."

❀

XIV
Mindfulness for Stress Management

Stress is a part of modern life, and it can take a toll on our physical and mental health if left unchecked. In this chapter, we will explore the role of mindfulness in stress management, and how it can help us achieve clarity and focus in our lives.

What is Mindfulness?

Mindfulness is the practice of being present and aware in the moment, without judgment. It involves paying attention to our thoughts, feelings, and physical sensations, and approaching them with compassion and non-judgment. The goal of mindfulness is to develop a deeper understanding of ourselves, and to cultivate a sense of peace and well-being.

Why Practice Mindfulness for Stress Management?

There are many benefits to practicing mindfulness for stress management, including:

Improved emotional regulation: Mindfulness can help us to regulate our emotions and reduce the negative impact of stress on our mental health.

Reduced physical symptoms of stress: Mindfulness has been shown to reduce physical symptoms of stress, such as headaches, muscle tension, and high blood pressure.

Increased resilience: Mindfulness can help us to build resilience and cope better with stress and difficult situations.

Improved focus and clarity: Mindfulness can help us to focus and concentrate more effectively, reducing distractions and increasing our ability to complete tasks.

How to Practice Mindfulness for Stress Management

Here are some tips for practicing mindfulness for stress management:

Start with a daily mindfulness practice: Set aside time each day for a mindfulness practice, such as meditation, yoga, or deep breathing.

Pay attention to your thoughts and feelings: When you notice feelings of stress or anxiety, take a moment to acknowledge them, and approach them with kindness and compassion.

Practice self-compassion: Treat yourself with kindness and understanding, and avoid negative self-talk.

Engage in physical activity: Regular physical activity, such as walking or yoga, can help reduce stress and improve overall well-being.

Get enough sleep: Adequate sleep is essential for reducing stress and improving overall health.

Connect with others: Spending time with friends and family, or participating in community activities, can help reduce feelings of stress and improve overall well-being.

In conclusion, mindfulness is a powerful tool for stress management, and it can help us to achieve clarity and focus in our lives. By taking the time to be present and aware in the moment, we can reduce stress and anxiety, improve our emotional regulation, and build resilience in the face of challenges. With regular practice, mindfulness can become a habit, helping us to live more mindfully and achieve greater well-being.

"Focus on the present and be mindful of your intentions to achieve clarity and purpose in life and create a meaningful existence."

❧

XV

Reaching Your Goals with Mindfulness

Setting and achieving our goals is an important part of living a fulfilling life. However, it can be easy to become overwhelmed by the pressures of daily life and lose sight of what is truly important to us. In this chapter, we will explore how mindfulness can help us to clarify our goals, stay focused, and achieve greater success.

The Benefits of Mindful Goal Setting

Mindful goal setting involves being present and aware as we set and work towards our goals. This approach helps to clarify our priorities, reduce stress, and increase our chances of success. Here are some of the key benefits of mindful goal setting:

Increased clarity and focus: Mindful goal setting helps us to clarify our priorities and focus on what is truly important to us.

Improved motivation: When we set goals that align with our values and aspirations, we are more likely to feel motivated and engaged.

Decreased stress: By breaking down our goals into manageable steps and focusing on the present moment, we can reduce stress and maintain a positive outlook.

Increased self-awareness: Mindful goal setting helps us to understand our strengths and weaknesses, and develop a deeper understanding of ourselves.

How to Practice Mindful Goal Setting

Here are some tips for practicing mindful goal setting:

Clarify your values and aspirations: Start by taking time to reflect on what is truly important to you, and what you want to achieve in your life.

Set specific and realistic goals: Set goals that are specific, measurable, and achievable, and be realistic about what you can accomplish in a given period of time.

Break down your goals into manageable steps: Divide your goals into smaller, achievable tasks, and focus on making progress towards your goals one step at a time.

Stay focused and present: Pay attention to your thoughts, feelings, and physical sensations as you work towards your goals, and stay focused on the present moment.

Practice self-compassion: Treat yourself with kindness and understanding when you encounter obstacles, and avoid negative self-talk.

Celebrate your successes: Celebrate your accomplishments, no matter how small, and take time to reflect on the progress you have made.

In conclusion, reaching your goals with mindfulness can help you to clarify your priorities, reduce stress, and increase your chances of success. By focusing on the present moment and engaging in self-reflection, you can develop a deeper understanding of yourself, and achieve greater clarity and focus as you work towards your goals. With regular practice, mindful goal setting can become a habit, helping you to live more mindfully and achieve greater happiness and fulfillment.

"Achieving clarity and focus requires a conscious effort to stay in the present moment."

&

OTHER BOOKS OF THE AUTHOR

1. The Moments When I Met God
2. Kashiyile Theertha Pathangal
3. Guru Gyan Vani
4. Abhiprerak Gita
5. Assi Se Jain Ghat Tak
6. Hopelessness of Arjuna
7. The Soul and It's True Nature
8. Sense of Action (Karma)
9. Action Through Wisdom
10. Action Through Wisdom
11. Theory And Practical of Every Action
12. Logical Understanding of The Supreme
13. The Imperishable Supreme
14. Yatra Nishadraj Se Hanuman Ghat Tak
15. Yatra Karnatak Ghat Se Raja Ghat Tak
16. Yatra Pandey Ghat Se Prayagraj Ghat Tak
17. Yatra Ranjendra Prasad Ghat Se Dattatreya Ghat Tak
18. Yaatrasindhiya Ghat Se Gwaliar Ghat Tak
19. Yatra Mangala Gauri Ghat Se Hanuman Gadhi Ghat Tak
20. Yatra Gaay Ghat Se Nishad Ghat Tak
21. Maa Ganga, Ghaten Evm Utsav
22. Ganga Arti Dev Deepavali Evam Any Utsav
23. Potentials of Digitalized India
24. Vedic Consciousness
25. A Brief Introduction to Vedic Science
26. Kashi Ke Barah Jyotirling
27. Impact Of Motivation
28. Let's Have a Milky Way Journey
29. Color Therapy in A Nutshell

OTHER BOOKS OF THE AUTHOR

30. Rigveda In a Nutshell
31. Yajurveda In a Nutshell
32. Samveda In a Nutshell
33. Atharva Veda In a Nutshell
34. Ayushman Bhava - Ayurveda
35. Srimad Bhagavad Gita and Upanishad Connection
36. Srimad Bhagavad Gita - An Attempt to Summarize Each Chapter.
37. Facts And Impact of Nakshatra
38. Astro Gems - Navaratna
39. Ekadashi - A Concise Overview
40. A Concise View of Hanuman Chalisa
41. Inspirational Gita
42. Nakshatraranyam
43. Summary of 18 Mahapuranas
44. Synopsis of 18 Upa Puranas
45. Rigvediya Upanishads
46. Shukla Yajurvediya Upanishads
47. Krishna Yajurvediya Upanishads
48. Samavediya Upanishads
49. Atharvavediya Upanishads
50. The Seven Great Sages
51. From Rocket Scientist to President Dr. Apj Abdul Kalam
52. The Visionary's Voice - Quotes of Dr. Apj Abdul Kalam
53. The Wisdom tf Swami Vivekananda: Insights and Inspiration from A Legendary Spiritual Teacher
54. Ayurvedic Remedies from The Garden
55. Sages and Seers
56. Rising Strong – Motivational Stories of Women
57. Beyond Flames -Mystery Stories of Funeral Ghat Manikarnika
58. The Origins of Tulsi: A Look at The Mythological Roots of The Plant"

OTHER BOOKS OF THE AUTHOR

59. The Holistic Cow: A Look at The Physical, Spiritual, and Cultural Importance of Cows in India
60. Arts of Healing
61. Exploring The Divine
62. Understanding Five Elements
63. The Etymology of Ram
64. Symbols of India
65. Voice of Change (About Speeches of Great Men)
66. She Speaks (About Speeches of Great Women)
67. Patriotism On Celluloid – Brief About Patriotic Films
68. The Music of Motivation: A Brief Guide to Inspirational Film Songs
69. Unlocking The Secrets of The Dashopanishads
70. A Cultural Mosaic
71. Ancient Traditions, Modern Minds
72. Ecos of Ancient Wisdom
73. Beneath The Surface
74. From Temples to Ashrams
75. Sages of The Subcontinent
76. The Art of Healling (Ayurveda, Yoga & Naturopathy)
77. Indian Kitchen
78. The Festivals of India
79. The Indian Epics Retold
80. The Power of Mantras
81. The Indian River Ganges
82. The Indian Architecture
83. Rites of Passage
84. The Indian Silk Road
85. The Indian Literature
86. The Indian Villages
87. The Indian Folks & Crafts
88. The Way of Buddha
89. The Ramayan of Tulsidas

OTHER BOOKS OF THE AUTHOR

90. Astrological Remedies
91. The Secret Power of Motivation
92. Secret Of Developing Your Inner Strength
93. The Secret Path to Motivation
94. The Art and Secret of Positive Thinking
95. The Secrets of Practicing Ethical Living
96. Indian Art and Painting
97. The Indian Herbalism
98. Bharatanatyam To Kathak
99. Exploring India's Astrological Remedies
100. The Indian Festival of Flowers
101. Indian Handicrafts
102. The Splashes of Joy – India's Colour Festival
103. The Indian Science of Astrology
104. The Indian Mythology
105. Path To Enlightenment
106. The Indian Spirituality for Children
107. Aromas Of India
108. The Secrets of Healthy Relationships
109. Ancestral Ties
110. The Indian Street Food
111. Discovering America
112. The Indian Textile
113. Listening To Motivational Speeches
114. Taste of India
115. A Cultural Journey Through Indian Nuptials
116. Motivational Quote for Change
117. Secret Strategies for Making Money
118. Secrets To Cultivate a Positive Mindset
119. A Tapestry of Cultures: Exploring India from Kashmir to Kanyakumari
120. Achieving Your Dreams with Resilience: Secret Strategies for Overcoming Obstacles

OTHER BOOKS OF THE AUTHOR

121. Innovative Start-ups - 25 Start-up Ideas To Spark Your Business Creativity
122. Export Management: Strategies for Global Success
123. Exporting From India - A Step by Step Guide
124. Finance Fundamentals: Mastering Financial Management for Business Success
125. Global Growth Strategies for International Business Development
126. Marketing Mastery: Unlocking the Secrets of Modern Marketing
127. Operations Mastery: Managing the Flow of Value in Business
128. Strategic Business Management: Navigating the Modern Business Landscape
129. Human Resource Management Strategies for Building and Managing a High-Performance Team
130. The Indian Landscapes and Nature: An Exploration of India's Natural Beauty and Diversity
131. The Indian Street Performances: A Cultural Exploration of India's Street Performances
132. Affirming Your Self-Worth: Strategies for Achieving Emotional Wellbeing
133. Cultivating Self-Discipline: Secrets Methods for Achieving Your Goals
134. Embracing Change: Strategies for Adapting to Life's Challenges
135. Embracing Your Uniqueness: Secret Strategies for Living an Authentic Life
136. Finding Motivation in Despondency: Coping with Difficult Times
137. Embracing Change
138. Learning To Love Yourself
139. Managing Time for Yourself

OTHER BOOKS OF THE AUTHOR

140. Unlock The Keys to Self-Motivation
141. Secret To Boost Confidence
142. Unlocking Your Potential: A Path to Inner-Strength & Success
143. Secrets To Develop Authentic Relationship
144. Secrets To Build a Successful Career
145. Secrets To Live with Gratitude
146. Secrets To Create a Life of Abundance
147. Secrets To Cultivate Self-Awareness
148. The Power of Helping Hands
149. Finding Your Passion
150. The Indian Mythical Creatures
151. The Indian Women Saints
152. The Wisdom of The Saints
153. The Indian Royalty: A Cultural and Historical Exploration of India's Maharajas and Their Kingdom
154. The Mystic Land: A Cultural and Spiritual Exploration of India
155. India's Spiritual Legacy – Discovering the Cultural and Religious Significance of Bhakti Yoga.
156. The Indian Folktales: An Exploration of India's Oral Folklore Traditions
157. Steeping In History: A Look at India's Iconic Tea Culture
158. The Indian Way of Life: An Exploration of The Philosophy and Practices Of Indian Culture
159. From Silence to Sound: A Cultural and Historical Study of Indian Cinema
160. Chronicles Of Indian Style: Tracing the Transformations of Traditional and Contemporary Fashion
161. Decorating India: A Journey Through the Traditions and Transformations of Home Design
162. Adornments Of India: A Journey Through the History and Artistry Behind Indian Jewelry

• 94 •

OTHER BOOKS OF THE AUTHOR

163. The Indian Royal Kitchens: A Gastronomic Journey Through the Kitchens of India's Maharajas
164. The Indian Sports: An Insight into The History and Significance of Indian Traditional Sports
165. The Indian Traditional Games: A Study of The Significance and Evolution of Indian Traditional Games
166. Secrets To Make Positive Choices: Strategies for Achieving Your Goals
167. Secrets To Motivate Yourself for Success Strategies for Reaching Your Goals
168. Secrets To Overcome Adversity: Strategies for Coping with Difficult Times
169. Secrets to Reach Your Goals with Positivity: Strategies for Achieving Your Dreams
170. The Creative Mind: An Exploration of the Secrets to Unleash Your Creativity
171. The Power of Positive Habits: Building Your Life on a Foundation of Success
172. The Secret and Power of Self-Belief: Overcoming Life Challenges with Confidence
173. Harnessing Your Inner Power: A Guide to Achieving Success
174. The Secret Art of Self-Care: Practicing Wellbeing and Resilience
175. Achieving Clarity and Focus: Strategies for Living Mindfully
176. Building Confidence Through Self-Love: A Guide to Achieving Self-Acceptance
177. Dealing with Difficult Emotions: Strategies for Achieving Emotional Well-Being
178. Developing Emotional Wellbeing: A Guide to Achieving Balance
179. Finding Balance in Your Life: Strategies for Achieving

Inner Peace
180. Finding Your Purpose: A Guide to Living an Authentic Life
181. Learning to Overcome Fear: A Guide to Achieving Your Goals
182. Mind Over Matter: Strategies for achieving Coherence and Concentration
183. Living with Intention: Strategies for Achieving Your Goals
184. Mastering Self-Compassion: A Guide to Nurturing Your Mind and Body
185. Mastering Self-Discipline: Strategies for Achieving Your Goals
186. Overcoming Negative Thinking: Strategies for Achieving Your Goals
187. Reclaiming Your Power: Strategies for Achieving Empowerment
188. Releasing Stress and Anxiety: A Guide to Achieving Balance
189. Setting Healthy Boundaries: Strategies for Protecting Yourself
190. Taking Control of Your Life: Strategies for Creating a Meaningful Future
191. Taking Responsibility for Your Life: Strategies for Achieving Self-Mastery
192. The Power of Positive Attitude: Strategies for Achieving Your Goals
193. Understanding Your Emotional Intelligence: Strategies for Living with Ease

CONTACT

DR. JAGADEESH PILLAI

MBA & PhD in Vedic Science

Four Times Guinness World Record Holder

Winner of Mahatma Gandhi Vishwa Shanti Puraskar and
Global Peace Ambassador

Gemology, Astro & Vastu Consultant - Spiritual Counselor

Consultant for designing World Record Ideas

Efficient Tarot Card Reader

9839093003

myrichindia@gmail.com

drjagadeeshpillai@facebook

drjagadeeshpillai@instagram

jagadeeshpillai@youtube

www. JAGADEESHPILLAI.com

ॐ

|| LOKAHA SAMASTHAHA SUKHINO BHAVANTU ||

Printed in the USA
CPSIA information can be obtained
at www.ICGtesting.com
LVHW031648071023
760446LV00001B/231